source to resource

FROM SUNSHINE TO LIGHT BULB

MICHAEL BRIGHT

Crabtree Publishing Company

www.crabtreebooks.com

Crabtree Publishing Company
www.crabtreebooks.com
1-800-387-7650

Published in Canada
Crabtree Publishing
616 Welland Avenue
St. Catharines, ON
L2M 5V6

Published in the United States
Crabtree Publishing
PMB 59051
350 Fifth Ave, 59th Floor
New York, NY 10118

Author: Michael Bright

Editorial director: Kathy Middleton

Freelance editor: Katie Woolley

Editors: Annabel Stones, Liza Miller, and Ellen Rodger

Designer: Rocket Design Ltd

Proofreader: Wendy Scavuzzo

Prepress technician: Samara Parent

Print and production coordinator: Katherine Berti

Published by Crabtree Publishing Company in 2017

First published in 2016 by Wayland
(A division of Hachette Children's Books)
Copyright © Wayland, 2016

Printed in Canada/072016/PB20160525

Photographs:
p 7 (top): NASA/Corbis; p 8 (bottom): NASA/GFSC/Science Photo Library; p 9 (top left), p 11 (bottom): NASA. p 13 (top): View Pictures/Getty; p 16: NASA; p 17 (top): Jochen Tack/imageBROKER/Corbis; p 19 (top): Perry Mastrovito/Corbis; p 23 (bottom): Yann Arthus-Bertrand/Corbis; p 25 (top): Chris Hellier/Corbis; p 25 (bottom): Floris Leeuwenberg/The Cover Story/Corbis; p 26: George Tiedemann/Corbis.

All other images and graphic elements courtesy of Shutterstock.

Illustrations:
Stefan Chabluk: p 6; p14-15; p 30

Every effort has been made to clear copyright. Should there be any inadvertent omission, please apply to the publisher for rectification.

The website addresses (URLs) included in this book were valid at the time of going to press. However, it is possible that contents or addresses may have changed since the publication of this book. No responsibility for any such changes can be accepted by either the author or the Publisher.

Library and Archives Canada Cataloguing in Publication

Bright, Michael, author
From sunshine to light bulb / Michael Bright.

(Source to resource)
Includes index.
Issued in print and electronic formats.
ISBN 978-0-7787-2707-1 (hardback).--
ISBN 978-0-7787-2711-8 (paperback).--
ISBN 978-1-4271-1817-2 (html)

1. Solar energy--Juvenile literature. 2. Renewable energy sources--Juvenile literature. I. Title.

TJ810.3.B74 2016   j333.792'3   C2016-902593-4
                                              C2016-902594-2

Library of Congress Cataloging-in-Publication Data

Names: Bright, Michael, author.
Title: From sunshine to light bulb / Michael Bright.
Description: St. Catharines, Ontario ; New York, New York : Crabtree Publishing, [2016] | Series: Source to resource | Includes index.
Identifiers: LCCN 2016016663 (print) | LCCN 2016016815 (ebook)
     ISBN 9780778727071 (reinforced library binding)
     ISBN 9780778727118 (pbk.)
     ISBN 9781427118172 (electronic HTML)
Subjects: LCSH: Solar energy--Juvenile literature. | Renewable energy sources--Juvenile literature.
Classification: LCC TJ810.3 .B74 2016 (print) | LCC TJ810.3 (ebook) | DDC 333.792/3--dc23
LC record available at https://lccn.loc.gov/2016016663

Contents

The Sun and our Earth.................. 4

The Sun................................. 6

Sunlight's journey to Earth 8

Electricity from sunlight 10

Solar panels.......................... 12

Electricity reaching homes...... 14

Electricity use 16

Electricity in the home 18

The light bulb....................... 20

Solar heating....................... 22

Solar towers and furnaces 24

The future of solar energy....... 26

Clean energy? 28

Further information................. 30

Glossary 31

Index 32

The Sun and our Earth

Solar energy is light and heat from the Sun. It is a renewable energy source because the Sun will never run out. Oil, coal, and natural gas are non-renewable energy sources because there is a limited supply of them. Someday, they will be completely used up.

The Sun and people

Energy from the Sun is vital for life on Earth. Plants need sunlight to grow, animals need to eat plants, and we need to eat plants and animals to survive. Without the Sun, there would be no plants, no animals, and no people.

Winds and waves

The Sun also powers the weather. It heats up the oceans and **atmosphere** closer to the **equator**. This hot air rises, and cold air from regions such as the North Pole rushes in to replace it. This produces winds that whip up waves.

Cows eat grass, and grass needs sunlight to grow.

Two other renewable energy sources are also generated by the Sun—wind and wave power.

Sun worship

Many ancient civilizations realized how important the Sun was to their survival, so they worshiped it. Ra was an ancient Egyptian sun god. He was always drawn with an eye like the glowing disc of the Sun. To the ancient Egyptians, Ra was the creator of all life.

Rain and rivers

Heat from the Sun causes clouds to form over the oceans. These clouds drop rain onto the land. The water flows into rivers that fill **reservoirs**. The movement of water out of reservoirs can be used to **generate** electricity. This is called **hydroelectric power**, and it is another renewable energy source that has its **origins** in the Sun.

The Sun

Our Sun is a star at the center of our solar system. It is 1.3 million times bigger than Earth, and consists mainly of two gases called hydrogen and helium.

Multi-layered Sun

The Sun is made up of many layers of gases. The temperature at the Sun's core is a staggering 27 million °F (15 million °C).

The *solar prominences* are great loops and fountains in the corona.

The *core* is the Sun's engine room, where solar energy is generated.

The *radiation zone* moves the heat quickly from the core to the next layer, the convection zone.

The *convection zone* is like a boiling pot. It moves the heat more slowly from the radiation zone to the photosphere.

The *corona* is the crown-like, wispy outer layer of the Sun that can be seen around the Sun's disc during a total eclipse.

The *photosphere* is the surface of the Sun, where light is released. Surprisingly, it can take several thousand years for heat to travel from the core to the Sun's surface.

The *chromosphere* is a layer of gas about 1,243 miles (2,000 km) thick above the Sun's surface. It sends out red light.

 (BRAINY BITS)

The Sun warms Earth, even though it is very far away.

Clever Copernicus

Before the 1500s, it was thought that Earth was the center of the universe and that the Sun revolved around it. All that changed in 1530 B.C.E. The Polish astronomer Nicolaus Copernicus said that Earth circles the Sun, which is the center of our solar system. He was right!

How the Sun works

Solar energy begins in the Sun's core. There, tiny **subatomic particles** slam together in a process known as nuclear fusion. This produces most of the heat and light given off by the Sun.

The Sun's life span

The Sun formed about 4.6 billion years ago from a vast cloud of gas and dust. Today, it is described as being middle-aged, so it is unlikely to change very much for another four billion years.

Sunlight's journey to Earth

The Sun is about 93 million miles (150 million km) away from Earth, so heat and light from the Sun must travel a great distance through space to reach us. But it does not take long. On average, sunlight completes the journey in 8 minutes and 20 seconds.

Energy through space

The journey may be quick but only a very small proportion of the Sun's energy actually reaches Earth. Even so, there is more solar energy reaching Earth every day than all the people on our planet could possibly use.

Reflected sunlight

Not all the sunlight that travels into Earth's atmosphere reaches its surface. About one third is reflected back into space and lost. All surfaces reflect sunlight, even a black road, but snow, ice, and the tops of clouds reflect the most.

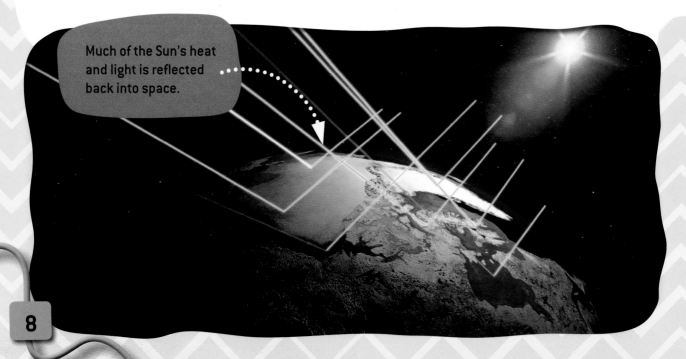

Much of the Sun's heat and light is reflected back into space.

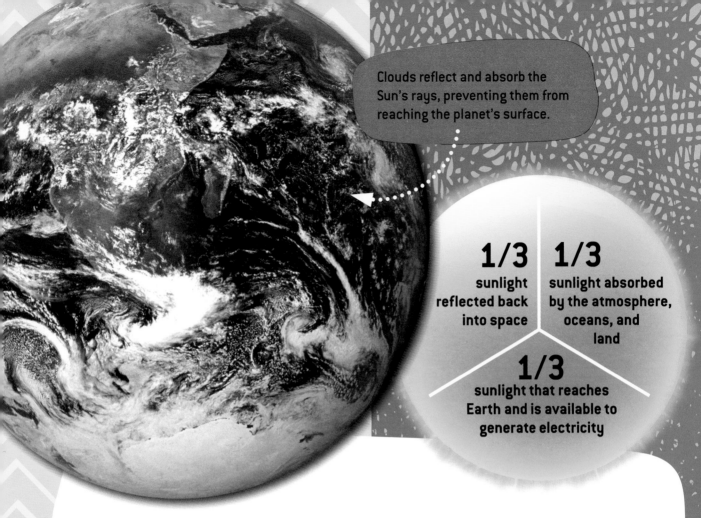

Clouds reflect and absorb the Sun's rays, preventing them from reaching the planet's surface.

1/3 sunlight reflected back into space

1/3 sunlight absorbed by the atmosphere, oceans, and land

1/3 sunlight that reaches Earth and is available to generate electricity

Absorbed sunlight

The atmosphere, oceans, and land **absorb** one third of the sunlight that is not reflected. In fact, they absorb more of the Sun's energy in one hour than the amount of energy we all use in an entire year. This means that only one third of the sunlight reaching Earth is available to generate electricity.

Worldwide impact

Power production is something all the countries of the world need to consider. Some forms of energy generation, such as coal, oil, or natural gas, produce a **greenhouse gas** called carbon dioxide. The more carbon dioxide that enters the atmosphere through these forms of power generation, the more the planet warms and polar and glacial ice melts. Less ice to reflect away sunlight means the planet warms even more. The reflection of sunlight is important to **global warming** and **climate change**. Environmentalists hope that solar power may one day replace these other forms of power generation, and help to slow down or even stop the ice melting. This, in turn, may reduce the impact of global warming.

Electricity from sunlight

Electricity can be converted directly from sunlight through solar cells. Modern solar cells were first invented in the 1900s, although the science behind them was actually discovered 100 years earlier.

How do they work?

Solar cells are made from thin layers of a chemical called silicon. When sunlight hits the silicon, it generates an **electric field** across the layers. The electricity created can be used to power electrical equipment.

When do they work?

Solar cells only work well when the Sun is shining. They are very dependent on the weather. On a cloudy day, they produce less electricity than on a sunny day, and they do not work at night.

Small solar cells like this can be found in calculators, but larger cells are used to make roof panels.

Many solar cells joined together are called solar panels or modules. Several panels joined together form an array that can produce a lot of electricity.

 Timeline

1839 Alexandre Edmond Becquerel discovers how sunlight can be **converted** into electricity.

1941 Russell Ohl invents the solar cell.

1954 Bell Labs produces the first useful silicon solar cell. Previous cells were inefficient.

1958 Vanguard I space satellite uses solar power in space for the first time.

1967 Soyuz 1 is the first manned spacecraft powered by solar cells.

1978 The first solar-powered calculators are invented.

2014 The solar-powered space probe, Philae, lands on a comet.

Solar-powered satellites

One of the first uses of solar cells was to power satellites in space. The early satellites were spheres with solar cells attached to the side. Later satellites and space probes, including the International Space Station, have large panels of solar cells resembling an aircraft's wings.

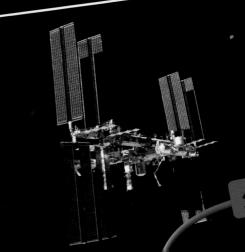

Solar panels

At first, solar cells were expensive to produce, but over the years they have become cheaper to make. This means people all over the world have begun to use solar panels on homes and buildings. Households can then generate their own electricity, and even sell some back to the energy companies.

Most homes have their solar panels on the roof.

Solar farms

People in some communities get together and use fields and other open spaces, such as factory roofs, for large arrays of solar panels. The panels can even swivel as they track the Sun across the sky.

Solar power stations

On a larger scale, solar power stations generate large amounts of electricity to be fed into the main electricity supply.

One of the largest solar power stations is the Solar Star in California. It has 1.7 million solar panels spread over 5 square miles (13 sq km) of the Mojave Desert.

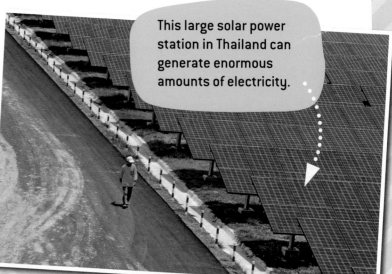

This large solar power station in Thailand can generate enormous amounts of electricity.

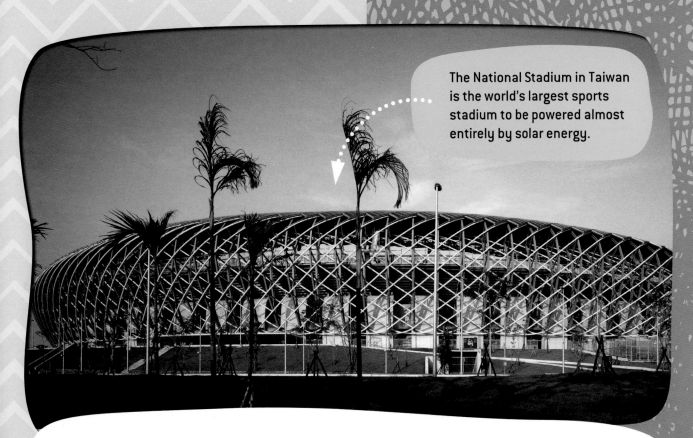

The National Stadium in Taiwan is the world's largest sports stadium to be powered almost entirely by solar energy.

Solar design

Some building designers are creating solar arrays that blend in with the environment. One of the first was the Solar Ark in Japan. The structure of 5,046 solar panels is built in the shape of a floating ark.

Solar architecture

Modern solar arrays are being included on important buildings, too. One of the most striking is the National Stadium in Taiwan. Its roof is covered in 8,844 solar panels, which would be enough to supply 1,000 homes with electricity if it was part of the national grid.

Solar on the street

Small solar panels are used to illuminate road traffic signs. Many have batteries to store the electricity generated during the day and light up the signs at night. Solar energy can also be used for street lighting in remote areas.

DID YOU KNOW?

If just a small area of the Sahara Desert was covered with solar panels, it could generate enough electricity for the entire world.

Electricity reaching homes

The electricity from solar panels, whether from household panels, solar farms, or solar power stations, is used directly by the home or fed into the local, regional, or national power supply. The power companies then distribute the power. It follows this process:

BRAINY BITS

3 Transformer substation
The electricity passes through a step-up transformer, which increases the **voltage**. A large amount of electricity at low voltage would be lost as heat. But this loss is reduced at higher voltages.

2 Inverter
Electricity from solar cells is **direct current** (DC) so it has to be converted into **alternating current** (AC) before it can be used. AC is used because it can be increased or decreased by a transformer.

1 Generator
The electricity is generated in various ways, including by solar farms and solar power stations.

4 Transmission lines

High-voltage transmission lines strung between towers or pylons carry the electricity to where it is needed. Cables can also run underground or along the bottom of oceans.

The longest

The world's longest undersea transmission line is between Norway and Netherlands in the North Sea. It is 360 miles (580 km) long.

5 Transformer substation

Here, a step-down transformer reduces the voltage to make it safe for use in the home.

The tallest

The world's tallest power transmission towers support overhead cables between Damao Island and Liangmao Island in China. The towers are 1,214 feet (370 m) tall.

6 Transmission lines

Low-voltage transmission lines carry electricity to a street. These cables run either overhead or underground.

Electricity use

Most of us take electricity for granted. We flick a switch and the lights turn on. Today, more and more people around the world are gaining access to electricity, which is creating an increase in demand.

Earth lights

It is only from the International Space Station orbiting Earth that the full extent of electricity use around the world can be seen. Cities across the globe blaze with artificial light, while less populated areas appear dark.

The grid

All the electricity **distribution lines** across countries and, in some cases, over entire continents, are interconnected. By sharing the electricity, power companies make sure it goes to where it is needed most. These networks are known as power grids.

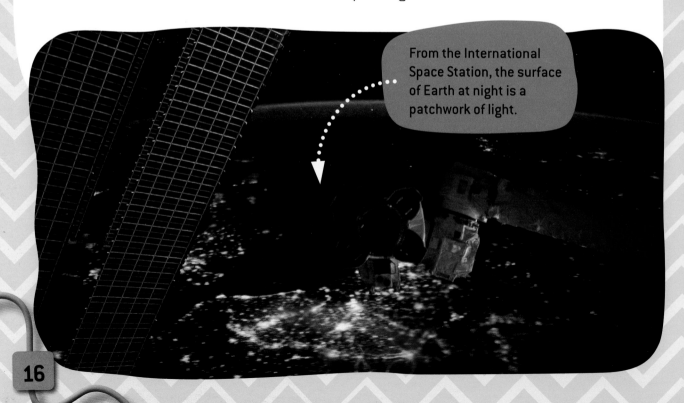

From the International Space Station, the surface of Earth at night is a patchwork of light.

Huge visual displays pinpoint where electricity is needed. The control room then directs it there.

Control rooms

The companies that run power grids control the flow of electricity from large control rooms. They direct electricity around their own region and send it out to, or bring it in from, other regions.

Peak demand

In many countries, electricity use is highest at 5:30 p.m. when homes, offices, and factories are all making heavy demands at the same time. Similar peaks occur on traditional feast days, such as Thanksgiving, when millions of electric ovens are cooking turkeys at the same time.

Super grids

Increasingly, countries are working together to ensure that the lights stay on. In Europe and North Africa, for example, there are plans to connect electricity networks to take advantage of the climate in different countries. Together, they will generate electricity from solar power, wind power, and hydroelectric power. North Africa gets more sunshine than Europe, and northern Europe has more wind and plenty of water, so the two regions can generate and swap electricity. The planned network is being called the SuperSmart Grid.

Electricity in the home

Most homes get their electricity supply from regional or national utility companies. Even homes that generate their own electricity through solar panels sometimes need to buy extra electricity from energy companies.

Electricity cables

When cables from an energy supplier or from solar panels enter a home, the electricity passes through several key stages.

Electricity meter

Electricity enters a house through an electricity meter. It records how much is being used, as well as how much extra electricty from the solar panels is being sold back to the energy company.

Fuse box or service panel

Electricity from the **mains** and solar panels passes through a box with **circuit breakers** or **fuses** that switch off the electricity if there is danger.

Household circuits

Inside the fuse box or service panel, electricity is routed to separate circuits, such as upstairs lights, downstairs lights, electric stove, upstairs sockets, and downstairs sockets. Each socket has its own emergency circuit breaker or fuse.

The service panel master switch turns the electricity supply on and off.

One fifth of electricity used in the home is for lighting.

Electrical circuits

On a lighting circuit, the electricity usually travels through wires hidden in the walls, floors, or ceilings. It might go directly to a light in the ceiling or on a wall. A plug-and-socket circuit allows you to connect an electrical device, such as a computer, to the main power supply.

DID YOU KNOW?

There are two main standards of electricity strength: 220 to 240 volts in Europe, and 120 volts in the U.S. and Canada.

Global plugs

Plugs and sockets are different all over the world. Some plugs have round pins, others have flat pins, and still others have rectangular pins. Here are just a few plugs and where they come from:

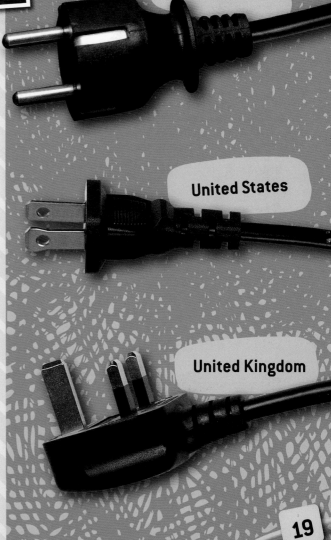

Europe

United States

United Kingdom

The light bulb

Before the late 1800s, lighting was fueled by gas and oil. Gas lamps lit city streets and oil lamps and candles lit homes. In 1879, that began to change when the first mass-produced electric light bulb was invented. It was called an incandescent light bulb.

How does it work?

The incandescent light bulb lights up when electricity passes through a wire **filament**. The filament heats up to a high temperature until it glows. It is protected within a glass bulb that contains a gas or a **vacuum**. Unfortunately, these kinds of light bulbs are not very efficient. More than 95 per cent of the energy produces heat rather than light.

Halogen

In 1882, the halogen light bulb was invented, but a household version was not available until 1959. In a halogen light bulb, the filament is surrounded by halogen gas. The filament lasts longer and glows brighter with a whiter light. It can also be much smaller and requires less electricity compared to an incandescent light bulb with the same brightness. It is often used in security lights outside houses.

Energy-saving light bulbs

Lighting accounts for nearly 20 percent of a household electricity bill, so many people are switching to compact fluorescent light bulbs (CFLs) and light emitting diodes (LEDs) to be less wasteful with electricity. Both are types of energy-saving light bulbs that are more efficient and use less electricity.

DID YOU KNOW?

In 1880, the electric light bulb was first used commercially, not in a home or in an office, but on a steamship—the **SS Columbia**.

Inventor of the light bulb

Thomas Edison was one of 24 scientists who invented the incandescent light bulb at about the same time. However, Edison is the person everyone remembers because his light bulb could be mass produced. He once said, "we will make electricity so cheap, that only the rich will burn candles."

Dim and bright

The brightness of a light bulb depends on its wattage. Usually, the higher the wattage, the brighter the bulb and the more electricity it uses. However, energy-saving light bulbs have a lower wattage than incandescent bulbs. They use less electricity, but are just as bright.

Solar heating

Solar panels use sunlight to generate electricity. Other solar devices can capture the Sun's heat and use it to heat water or air.

Solar water heating

The most common form of solar heating is the solar water heating system. It consists of a panel containing thin tubes filled with water, which is usually placed on the roof of a house. The Sun warms the water in the pipes and it is then sent to an **insulated** storage tank. More pipes may connect the tank to the house's central heating and hot water systems to warm rooms and heat water for household use. In warmer climates, solar hot water can provide 85 percent of a home's hot water needs.

There are two types of solar thermal panels: a flat plate panel with tiny tubes, and a larger tube version, like these, from which the air has been removed to reduce heat loss.

Buildings absorb heat from the Sun, which can be used to help warm the building.

Solar air heating

Special heat-absorbent materials can absorb the Sun's heat. The stored heat can be used to heat air being sucked into a building. A large panel or even an entire wall on the sunny side of a building might be used to absorb the Sun's heat. The warmed air is then pumped around the building in the heating systems.

Solar building design

Many modern buildings are being designed to maximize or minimize the Sun's energy. The walls, windows, and floors collect, store, and distribute solar energy as heat in the winter, yet they make sure that less heat is absorbed in the summer. Large windows are a simple way to absorb heat in winter, and shutters keep the Sun out in summer.

Danish island

The world's largest solar water heating systems are not found in a hot desert, but on the Danish island of Ærø. There, solar energy accounts for 30 percent of the island's annual heating needs, and this rises to 100 percent between June and August. Giant wind **turbines** provide 50 percent of its electricity, so the island gains most of its energy through renewable resources.

Solar towers and furnaces

Solar towers are used to capture the Sun's energy to heat water and generate electricity. Solar furnaces concentrate that energy to heat up furnaces to high temperatures.

How do they work?

Both these systems use mirrors that track the Sun across the sky and focus it on special towers. It works in a similar way to burning a hole in paper by focusing light on it through a magnifying glass.

Solar towers

A large number of flat mirrors focus sunlight onto a solar power tower. Inside the tower, a special heat-carrying fluid is heated to 932 °F (500 °C). This is pumped to a boiler and the heat is used to produce steam. The steam drives a turbine that generates electricity.

All the mirrors direct the sunlight at the central solar tower, which glows white-hot.

Solar furnaces

Solar furnaces use curved mirrors to heat chemicals up to very high temperatures. In the Pyrenees, a mountainous region in Europe, a solar furnace was built in a specific location because the area has about 300 sunny days a year.

Solar barbecues and ovens

Small, portable solar barbecues and ovens are being used in remote areas of poorer countries. They concentrate the Sun's rays to cook food and boil water, without the need to light fires and burn wood.

Solar bowl

At Auroville in India, a large solar bowl is used as a solar kitchen. The huge bowl-shaped mirror focuses sunlight on to a cylindrical boiler, heating the water inside to 302 °F (150 °C). The steam produced is enough to cook two meals a day for 1,000 people.

Curved mirrors focus sunlight onto a solar furnace in the Pyrenees. It can reach temperatures as high as 6,332 °F (3,500 °C).

The future of solar energy

Solar power has a bright future. Today, most solar panels and arrays supply electricity to homes, offices, and factories, but scientists and engineers are exploring many other ways to make use of solar power.

Cars

The first solar-powered car appeared in 1962. It was a converted 1912 electric car with a solar panel on the roof. Since then, engineers have experimented with cars powered by the Sun and solar energy batteries that store electricity at night. There are even solar sports car races!

Solar-powered cars can reach 55 mph (89 kph).

Boats

Solar panels have been used on boats to power electrical equipment, such as radios and navigation lights. Engineers are also developing boats that have solar-powered engines rather than engines that run on gas or diesel fuel. One of the most spectacular is the MS Tûranor *PlanetSolar*. It cruised around the world, powered by a huge array of solar cells on its deck.

Trains

In India, railway cars have solar panels on the roof to power the train's lighting. In Arizona, a company has plans to design and build a solar-powered train. The 220 mph (354 kph) *Solar Bullet* train will travel on electricity produced by solar panels which will be positioned above the train.

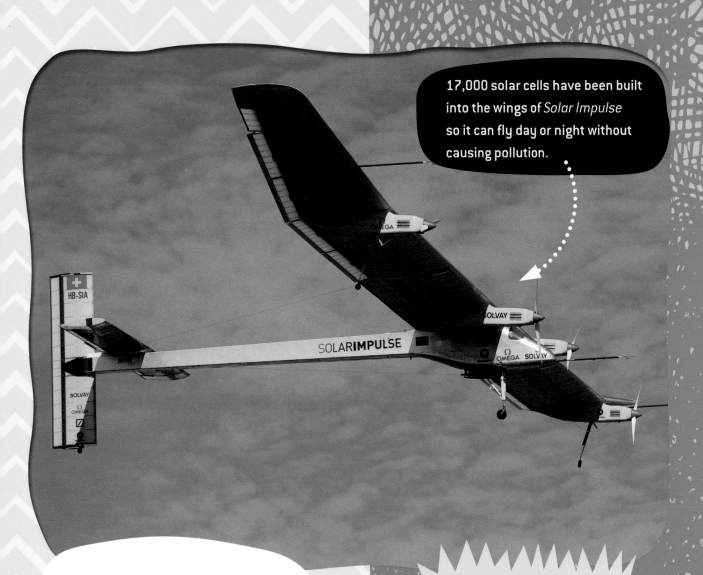

17,000 solar cells have been built into the wings of *Solar Impulse* so it can fly day or night without causing pollution.

Planes

Solar Impulse I and II are experimental solar-powered planes that have made record-breaking journeys across the world. *Solar Impulse* II's wings are covered with lightweight solar panels. These drive electric motors that turn the propellors.

Sun tower in space

Looking to the future, the ideal place to capture sunlight to generate electricity would be in space, using human-made satellites. There are no clouds to get in the way, and the satellite could be permanently facing the Sun. The electricity could be beamed down to collecting stations on Earth.

Clean energy?

There are many benefits to using solar power, but there are drawbacks as well. Decision-makers must weigh the pros and cons.

Against solar power

- Solar power depends on the weather. The Sun is not out all of the time.

- Solar power is limited to daylight hours, unless there is the large scale storage of electricity, for example, in expensive batteries.

- Solar installations can be expensive and do not make the same amount of power as oil, gas, coal, or nuclear power stations.

- Vast amounts of land are required for large-scale solar arrays.

- The manufacturing of solar cells creates greenhouse gases that contribute to climate change.

This is a traditional coal-fired power station.

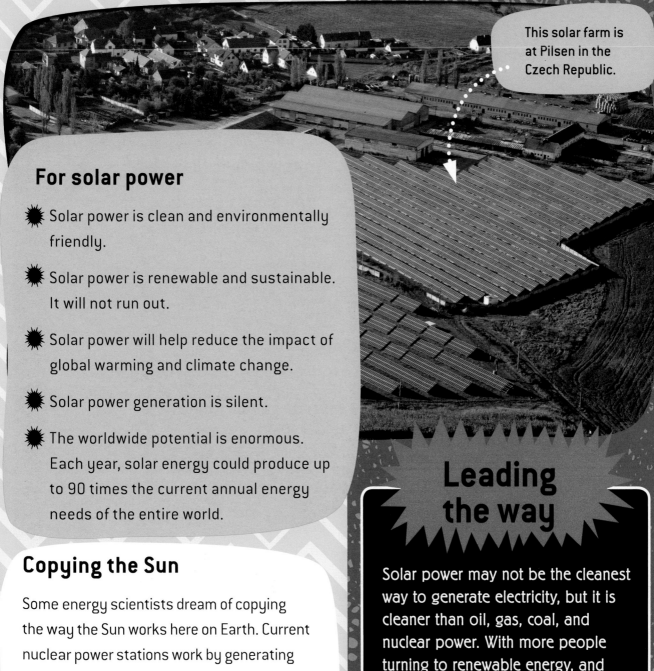

This solar farm is at Pilsen in the Czech Republic.

For solar power

* Solar power is clean and environmentally friendly.

* Solar power is renewable and sustainable. It will not run out.

* Solar power will help reduce the impact of global warming and climate change.

* Solar power generation is silent.

* The worldwide potential is enormous. Each year, solar energy could produce up to 90 times the current annual energy needs of the entire world.

Copying the Sun

Some energy scientists dream of copying the way the Sun works here on Earth. Current nuclear power stations work by generating heat from splitting the **atom**, a process called fission, but the by-product is hazardous **radioactive waste**. If scientists can join atoms in a process called fusion, which is what happens inside the Sun, large scale energy production would be cleaner and safer than nuclear power generation. The problem is that fusion power is very difficult to achieve.

Leading the way

Solar power may not be the cleanest way to generate electricity, but it is cleaner than oil, gas, coal, and nuclear power. With more people turning to renewable energy, and more countries determined to lower their use of **fossil fuels**, solar energy could become the leading way to generate electricity. The International Energy Agency predicts that by 2060, solar power could account for one third of the world's energy needs.

Further information

BOOKS

Eco-Works: How a Solar-Powered Home Works by Robyn Hardyman, Franklin Watts, 2015

Energy from the Sun by James Bow, Crabtree Publishing, 2016

Green Energy by Molly Aloian, Crabtree Publishing, 2014

The Sun by Reagan Miller, Crabtree Publishing, 2012

WEBSITES

Visit this website for more information about solar power:

www.eschooltoday.com/energy/renewable-energy/solar-energy.html

More facts about renewable energy sources can be found here:

www.eia.gov/kids/energy.cfm?page=solar_home-basics

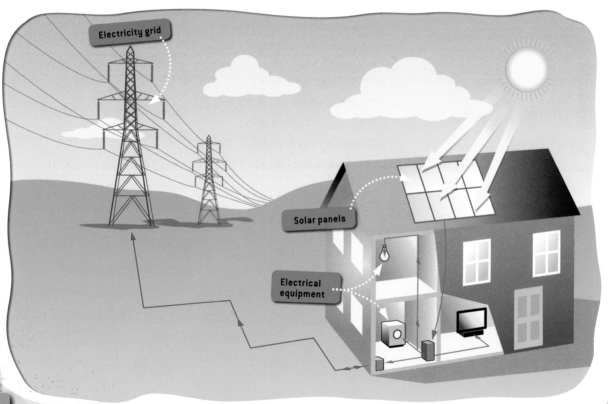

Glossary

absorb To take in or soak up

alternating current An electric current that reverses its direction many times a second

atmosphere The layer of gases that surrounds Earth

atom The smallest part of a chemical element that can exist

circuit breaker An automatic device for stopping the flow of electricity

climate change A process in which the environment changes. This can occur naturally, or it can be caused by human activity.

converted Changed

direct current An electric current flowing in one direction only

distribution line The cable that carries electricity around the country

electric field A region with a force generated by electricity

equator An imaginary line around the middle of Earth

filament A thin wire in a light bulb

fossil fuel A fuel made from the remains of ancient plants and animals

fuse A safety device in which a filament melts and breaks an electric circuit if the current exceeds a safe level

generate To produce or create

global warming An increase in the global temperature due mainly to increased levels of carbon dioxide in the atmosphere

greenhouse gas A gas that absorbs infrared radiation and traps it in the atmosphere, which contributes to climate change

hydroelectric power The electricity generated from the movement of water

insulated Describes something separated by a material that prevents heat, electricity, or sound from leaking out

mains The main distribution system for electrical power in a building

origins The point or place where something begins

radioactive waste Any material contaminated by radioactivity

reservoir An artificial lake to store water

subatomic particle The unit of matter smaller than a hydrogen atom

turbine A machine in which a wheel fitted with fins is made to revolve by a fast-moving stream of air, steam, water, or gas

vacuum A space without any matter

voltage A measure of the electrical force that would drive an electric current between two points

Index

C

circuits 18, 19
climate change 9, 28, 29
coal 4, 9, 28, 29

E, G

electric fields 10
electricity 4, 9, 10–21, 23, 24, 26–9
global warming 9, 29

H, L, M

hydroelectric power 5, 17
light bulbs 20, 21
mains electricity 18

N, O

national grids 13, 16–18
natural gas 4, 9
nuclear fusion 7, 29
oil 4, 9, 20, 28, 29

S

solar arrays 11–13, 14, 26, 28
solar cells 10–12, 14, 26–28
solar farms 12, 14, 29
solar furnaces 24–25
solar heating 22–23
solar modules 11
solar panels 11, 12–13, 14, 18, 22, 26, 27
solar power stations 12, 14
solar system 6, 7
solar thermal panels 22
solar towers 24–25, 27

W

wave power 4, 5
wind power 4, 5, 17
wind turbines 23